Ursula Andress, born on 19th March 1 Canton of Bern, Switzerland, is a film a model and sex symbol, who's appeared Italian films. She's best known for her b Bond girl Honey Ryder, in the first James ... movie, Dr. No (1962), having later starred as Vesper Lynd in the Bond film Casino Royale (1967). Ursula's other movies included Fun in Acapulco, She, The 10th Victim, The Blue Max, Perfect Friday, The Sensuous Nurse, The Mountain of the Cannibal God, The Fifth Musketeer and Clash of the Titans.

Andress, the 3rd of 6 children, with a brother and 4 sisters, is the daughter a German couple, Anna, a landscape gardener, and Rolf Andress, a German diplomat, who was expelled from Switzerland for political reasons, having disappeared during World War II. Ursula attended school in the Swiss capital Berne until she was 16, having become fluent in French, German and Italian. She studied art in Paris for a year then went to Rome, where she had jobs including being a children's nanny.

Andress was at a party when she met a film producer, who offered her a screen test for a role in an Italian movie, in which she was successful, appearing in The Sins of Casanova (1955), starring her later Bond ally Gabriele Ferzetti. Ursula followed it with An American in Rome (1954), starring Alberto Sordi then La catena dell'odio (1955), being seen by a Hollywood executive, who persuaded her to try her luck in Hollywood.

Andress arrived in Hollywood during January 1955 then in March she was signed to a 7-year contract with Paramount Pictures, starting on $287 / week. However, the contract didn't lead to any acting roles due to her inadequate English, Ursula later saying "I spent most of my time watching old Marlene Dietrich movies".

Andress got a lot of publicity when dating James Dean, shortly before the actor's death then bought herself out of her contract, it being announced during March 1956 that she'd signed to Columbia Pictures. However, Ursula made no films for them either, although she became Miss World Trade of 1956. She stayed in Hollywood because she married actor John Derek the following year, it then being announced during 1959 that she and Derek would star in High Variety, but again no movie was made.

Andress returned to the screen during 1962 in an episode of Thriller, "La Strega", with Alejandro Rey, soon after becoming internationally famous as Honey Ryder, a shell diver and James Bond's object of desire in Dr. No (1962), the first Bond movie. In what became an iconic moment in cinematic and fashion history, Ursula rose out of the Caribbean Sea in a white bikini, with a large diving knife on her hip.

Due to the heavy Swiss-German accent of Andress, her character's voice was provided by Nikki van der Zyl, while the calypso was sung by Diana Coupland. The scene made her a "quintessential" Bond girl, Ursula later saying that she owed her career to the white bikini: "This bikini made me into a success. As a result of starring in Dr. No as the first Bond girl, I was given the freedom to take my pick of future roles and to become financially independent."

The bikini she wore in the film sold at auction during 2001 for £41,125. The white web belt she was wearing was donated by sailors from HMS Troubridge, watching on the set when Andress realized something was missing from her outfit, the belt being a part of the full dress uniform of the Royal Navy. In a UK Survey by Channel 4 during 2003, her entrance in Dr. No was voted #1 in "the 100 Greatest Sexy Moments". Ursula won the Golden Globe Award for New Star of the Year in 1964, for her appearance in the film.

Andress followed Dr. No by playing the female lead in an Elvis Presley musical, Fun in Acapulco (1963) then was billed after Frank Sinatra, Dean Martin and Anita Ekberg in '4 for Texas' (1963), her casting having led to the title being changed from Two for Texas, both movies attracting big audiences.

Less successful was a film Ursula starred in alongside Derek, Nightmare in the Sun (1965). That year nude photographs of her from Nightmare in the Sun were published in Playboy, the first of 7 times she was featured in the magazine over the next 15 years. When asked why she'd agreed to do the Playboy shoot, Andress replied coolly, "Because I'm beautiful."

Ursula was cast in the title role of She (1965), playing an immortal queen, for Hammer Films and Seven Arts Productions, shot in England and Israel, which Andress agreed to make as part of a two-picture deal with Seven Arts. It was a hit at the box office, but she decided not to appear in the sequel, The Vengeance of She (1967).

Ursula was then cast in a supporting role in the comedy What's New Pussycat? (1965) for producer Charles K. Feldman, which was a huge hit. That year she also traveled to France to play Jean-Paul Belmondo's love interest, in Up to His Ears (1965), which was popular in that country. She and Belmondo became romantically involved, leading to her and Derek breaking up, although they remained close friends. Andress moved to Paris to live with Belmondo, which became her home for the next 7 years.

Ursula starred opposite Marcello Mastroianni in the science fiction movie, The 10th Victim (1965), in Italy, before returning to Hollywood to play George Peppard's love interest in the World War One film, The Blue Max (1966), another box office hit. Andress then made her second movie for Seven Arts, with John Derek, who again starred and directed, Once Before I Die (1966), shot in the Philippines. The Bond satire Casino Royale

(1967) followed, produced by Charles K. Feldman, in which Ursula played Vesper Lynd, an occasional spy who persuaded Evelyn Tremble, played by Peter Sellers, to carry out a mission.

It was a big box office hit, for which her fee was £200,000. The next year Andress appeared alongside fellow former Bond girl Claudine Auger in Anyone Can Play (1968) in Italy, for director Luigi Zampa. She then traveled to Africa to make The Southern Star (1969) with George Segal, which was a hit in the UK. She went on to appear nude or semi-nude in nearly all of her film roles from 1969 - 1979, being nicknamed "Ursula Undress".

Andress travelled to England to star in Perfect Friday (1970), a heist movie starring Stanley Baker and David Warner then the following year she appeared in Red Sun (1971), a Western shot in Spain with an international cast, including Charles Bronson, Toshiro Mifune and Alain Delon. Ursula said during 1972, "I think my image, especially to Americans, is that of a femme fatale, a man-eating woman. I'm not empty headed or calculating and cool, but maybe my looks give that impression. I'm disciplined in my doings and undisciplined in my emotions. I can't control the things I feel or hide my feelings."

Andress starred in some action films, Motel of Fear (1973, Loaded Guns (1974), and Africa Express (1975), followed by the title role in The Sensuous Nurse (1975) then appeared in a comedy with another former Bond girl, Barbara Bouchet, Spogliamoci così, senza pudor... (1976). Ursula also played Joséphine de Beauharnais in the swashbuckling spoof The Loves and Times of Scaramouche (1976) with Michael Sarrazin that year, before starring in a sequel to Africa Express, Safari Express (1976), then made another movie with Marcello Mastroianni, Double Murder (1978).

Closing out the '70s, Andress appeared in the cult favourite Slave of the Cannibal God (1978) with Stacy Keach, Tigers in

Lipstick (1979) for Luigi Zampa, and The Fifth Musketeer (1979), playing Louise de La Vallière. She started the new decade by playing Aphrodite in 1981's Clash of the Titans, in which she worked with Laurence Olivier. Andress had a relationship with leading man Harry Hamlin during the making of the film, who became the father of her child.

Ursula portrayed Mabel Dodge in the adventure-drama movie Red Bells (1982), having also guest starred on shows including Manimal and The Love Boat. In France she was in Liberté, égalité, choucroute (1985), while on TV she appeared in the Emmy-winning miniseries Peter the Great during 1986. She then joined the cast of the primetime soap opera Falcon Crest for a 3-episode arc in 1988 as an exotic foreigner, who assisted David Selby in rescuing Dana Sparks from a white slave ring.

Andress was also in Big Man – The Diva (1988) that year with Bud Spencer and Man Against the Mob: The Chinatown Murders (1989). From the start of the 1990s, her acting appearances have become less frequent, Ursula having appeared in Klassäzämekunft (1990), The Cave of the Golden Rose 3 (1993), The Cave of the Golden Rose 4 (1994) and Cremaster 5 (1995).

Andress was chosen by Empire magazine as one of the "100 Sexiest Stars in film history during 1995." Her last role to date was playing "Madonna" in the low-budget Swiss feature Die Vogelpredigt oder Das Schreien der Mönche (de) (The Bird Preachers) during 2005. Ursula then appeared in the documentary Masterpiece or Forgery? The Story of Elmyr De Hory in 2008.

Andress dated film icon James Dean shortly before his death during 1955. That same year, she began an affair with actor/director John Derek, a married father-of-two who walked out on his wife, Pati Behrs, and their family, to be with 19-year-old Ursula. They wed during 1957 in Las Vegas, before separating in 1963 then divorcing during 1966.

Andress had romantic relationships with Jean-Paul Belmondo, Ryan O'Neal and Fabio Testi, followed by American actor Harry Hamlin whom she met on the set of Clash of the Titans during 1979. She gave birth to their son, Dimitri Hamlin, on 19th May 1980, at the age of 44 then moved into her close friend Linda Evans' Coldwater Canyon home until hers was ready. Although they got engaged the couple never married, Hamlin having broken up with her during 1983.

Filmography

Film Year Role Notes

Un americano a Roma 1954 Astrid uncredited
La catena dell'odio 1955 N/A
Le avventure di Giacomo Casanova 1955
Thriller 1962 Luana TV series; episode: "La Strega"
Dr. No 1962 Honey Ryder Golden Globe Award for New Star of the Year - Actress
Fun in Acapulco 1963 Marguerita Dauphin
4 for Texas 1963 Maxine Richter
Nightmare in the Sun 1965 Marsha Wilson
She 1965 Ayesha
What's New Pussycat? 1965 Rita
Up to His Ears 1965 Alexandrine Pinardel
The 10th Victim 1965 Caroline Meredith
The Blue Max 1966 Countess Kaeti von Klugermann
Once Before I Die 1966 Alex
Casino Royale 1967 Vesper Lynd/007
Anyone Can Play 1968 Norma
The Southern Star 1969 Erica Kramer

Perfect Friday 1970 Lady Britt Dorset
Red Sun 1971 Cristina
Loaded Guns 1974 Nora Green
Stateline Motel 1975 Michelle Nolton
Africa Express 1975 Madeleine Cooper
The Sensuous Nurse 1975 Anna
The Loves and Times of Scaramouche 1976 Joséphine de Beauharnais
Sex with a Smile II 1976 Marina
Safari Express 1977 Miriam
Double Murder 1978 Principessa Dell'Orso
The Mountain of the Cannibal God 1978 Susan Stevenson
The Fifth Musketeer 1979 Louise de La Vallière
Tigers in Lipstick 1979 The Stroller/The Widow
Clash of the Titans 1981 Aphrodite
Red Bells 1982 Mabel Dodge
Manimal 1983 Karen TV series
The Love Boat 1983 Carole Stanton TV series
Liberté, Égalité, Choucroute (fr) 1985 Marie Antoinette
Peter the Great 1986 Athalie TV mini-series
Falcon Crest 1988 Madame Malec TV series
Il Professore – Diva 1988 Susy Kaminski TV movie
Klassezämekunft (de) 1988 Agnes
Man Against the Mob: The Chinatown Murders 1989 Betty Starr TV movie
Ti ho adottato per simpatia 1991 TV movie
Fantaghirò 3 1993 Xellesia TV movie
Fantaghirò 4 1994 Xellesia TV movie
Alles gelogen 1996
Cremaster 5 1997 Queen of Chain
Die Vogelpredigt oder Das Schreien der Mönche (de) 2005 Madonna
Masterpiece or Forgery? The Story of Elmyr De Hory documentary 2008.

"Happy Birthday Ursula Andress". 18th May 2006. On the occasion of the inauguration of the Swiss Consulate General in

Scotland, Ursula Andress celebrated her 70th birthday on board the Royal Yacht Britannia, moored at the Ocean Terminal in Edinburgh.

Ursula Andress sat in the middle of the party, looking every inch the glamour puss, a buzz in the room surrounding her table, flashbulbs popping with the paparazzi unable to get enough of her. Even at 66, she still knew how to toss back her hair, making grown men look. Andress was there to help launch Edmond Avakian's new London jewellery store, being the perfect choice for the occasion.

Winner of Maxim's Icon award, while being ranked # 19 in Playboy's "100 Sexiest Stars of the Century," Ursula's name forever evoked the image of a vision rising from the sea to meet James Bond in Dr No but now she'd got her feet planted firmly on dry land: "I was lucky to earn money easily, but I invested it carefully and now I'm happy I did, because then I had the responsibility of raising my child as a single mother." Andress adored her son Dimitri, 22, from her relationship with actor Harry Hamlin.

In keeping with her reputation as a thoroughly autonomous woman, Ursula did all her own investing, without advice from any professionals, having chosen to spread her risk across gold, stocks and property: "I do it myself and maybe I have less money because of that, but at least I know what I have. I'm currently very, very conservative. My stocks were doing marvellously until two years ago, but then ..." Andress used both hands to indicate the downturn that followed, " ... it went crazy for me like everybody. Worldcom did very well and were my favourite - until they were a disaster."

Ursula grew up during the war in Berne, Switzerland, the 3rd of 6 children to a Swiss mother and a German father. Her father was expelled from Switzerland for political reasons, so her grandfather, a garden designer, took the role of guardian. "My childhood was incredibly unique, almost like the 17th-century. My grandfather was a very strict man and we lived in a big house with a big nursery. I had to work very hard in the greenhouses and cleaning the furnaces out at night - I worked a lot. It taught me respect and discipline, which is such an enormous lesson. It gave me the strength to confront any obstacle in life."

Paramount gave Andress a contract as a young hopeful at the age of 18, having begun a rigid training regime. She was sent to classes in English, diction, local etiquette, acting skills and general personal development but after a year, the Paramount boss gave up, so she bought herself out of the contract.

"I was so happy, the money never really meant very much to me, it was the quality of life I liked. My independence is very important. Freedom is my greatest extravagance - I don't allow myself to spend carelessly. Money brings you happiness, I don't deny it. It helps everyone, but I think we shouldn't abandon values. I can't be a slave to anything - except perhaps a little bit to a man."

Ursula wed director John Derek during 1957, who for the 8 years they were together made it his job to develop her career, as he later did with Bo Derek. Her big break came in 1962, when she starred in Dr No. Andress had a big impact in the days before the sexual revolution, when leading ladies were usually expected to be soft and submissive, having helped hurry along a change in attitude, by presenting the image of a woman as fiercely independent as she was desirable.

After that, Ursula went on to a spectacularly trashy career, with films including Slave of the Cannibal God and The Sensuous Nurse, although she also appeared in other more worthwhile movies, including Casino Royale, a spoof Bond film and 'She': "I was forced to do She. It was a very cheap Hammer film and the only thing I adored was the costumes. I was just lucky to look good in it, because they photographed me beautifully."

Andress was now dividing her time between her homes in Rome and the U.S. "I've had a very fabulous life and if I had to go tomorrow I wouldn't mind, but for the children who haven't had their turn yet, I feel sorry that we made a very big mess of this world."

Lottery: Ursula didn't think £10m went very far anymore. She loved houses, of which she had "a few", and furniture, so she'd probably spend it on that.

Ideal holiday: Somewhere nobody else was. Andress loved nature and being alone, though she'd happily take a man along. Tipping: If there was good service it was worth it, but if not it shouldn't be expected.

Investment advice: Put it in property. "Right now the world situation is critical and values are uncertain. It's very difficult to trust in business and stocks."

Domestic division of responsibility: "I've always lived with artists, who are people that don't think about money, so it was always down to me." That sounded very careless of a lot of famous names, including James Dean, Marcello Mastroianni, Dean Martin, Elvis Presley ...

Best buy: The bikini she'd worn in Dr No. Ursula made it herself, being unhappy with what they had on set. After she'd rescued it from her attic, it had auctioned the previous year for £41,125 - ten times more than the price fetched for one of Madonna's studded bras, but the real value to her was the rest of her career.

Mistakes: Giving money to friends to invest in business ideas that never amounted to anything. "When somebody asks you, it is hard to say no," said Andress.

The problem with osteoporosisis is that many women with the condition go undiagnosed and even in those cases that are detected, many, like Ursula Andress, don't take their medication - with serious results. Ursula had been unaware of how serious the disease could be when it was detected during a routine health check in the year 2000.

A scan revealed the bones in her hips were showing early signs of weakening, but she disregarded the diagnosis, saying she wasn't an obvious candidate for osteoporosis, being physically fit and eating calcium-rich foods: 'I've always been sporty and had lots of exercise, I've never smoked, I've always eaten well, including dairy, and drink wine only with a meal. While my mother had a hip replacement, she didn't fracture a hip to my knowledge and she lived to be 96.

True, I was post-menopausal, but otherwise had none of the risk factors. I didn't think someone like me - a former Bond girl who from 7am until late is go, go, go, who eats well and walks miles every day - would get this disease. Foolishly, I refused to take the diagnosis seriously. The doctor told me to take a daily pill to help stop my bones from getting any weaker and to take calcium to help keep the bones strong, but I'm the world's worst pill-taker, always have been. About 4 years ago I was in India, when I caught pneumonia. I pleaded with the doctor to give me the shortest dose of antibiotics possible, because I knew otherwise I wouldn't finish the course.

'With the osteoporosis pills, I would think: "I will take it later" - and it would get later and later, and days passed without me taking the medication. Within a few months I gave up altogether and just took calcium when I remembered. I thought I would be fine, especially as I had no pain and was still swimming and walking miles every day, which I thought would keep my bones strong. Besides, by drinking a bit more milk and eating a bit more cheese I thought my bones would improve. I was totally wrong. By not taking my medication I've put myself at great risk.'

Andress had her first full medical since her diagnosis during 2008, having been horrified when the doctors told her that a scan indicated that her bones had greatly deteriorated: 'The doctor told me that unless I took my medicine, I would definitely fracture my hip within the next few years, even a stumble would be enough for this to happen. It was a total wake-up call for me. I've always been so healthy, and the idea that just going about my day-to-day life could put me at risk was a real shock. Bones don't heal themselves with a sticking plaster; this was serious. That scared me a lot'.

Ursula said she would rather die if her condition stopped her from being active: 'I am passionate about life and the things I love, such as my garden at my home in Italy, tending to my animals and seeing my friends. It would devastate me if I couldn't enjoy those things because my body had let me down. I would also feel so embarrassed if I had to become dependent on anyone to help me with day-today life. I adore my son and he is good to me, but I would hate to become reliant on him. It made me realise I had to take this condition seriously and start taking medication.'

The most common treatment for osteoporosis was with bisphosphonates - drugs that slowed down the rate at which old bone was absorbed and helped the cells that make new bone work more efficiently. These were normally taken as a daily, weekly or monthly pill, but to be effective, the medication needed to be taken regularly and at specific times of the day - generally an hour before food, which could become problematic, stated Professor David Reed, chairman of the National Osteoporosis Society.

There were many women like Andress who neglected to take their medication, the latest survey having found that 70% didn't take it regularly - almost half of them intentionally, because of the fear of side-effects including irritation to the gut or because they were confused by the instructions. However, generally, it was never too late for properly taken medication to make a difference.

'You're not going to be able to get the bones back to the way they used to be, but you can retain their strength and stop them from getting worse,' said Prof. Reed. Because of her blind spot with regards to pill-taking, Ursula and her doctor had agreed that she could have a once-a-year treatment. Zoledronic acid, a form of bisphosphonate, was given during an annual 15-minute infusion. Studies had found that it could reduce the risk of a hip fracture by more than 40% and a spinal fracture by more than 70%.

Although available in Britain, it was more expensive than other treatments, generally being given only to those for whom other medications hadn't worked or who'd had side-effects. 'People should discuss with their doctor if they don't think they're on the right medication,' said Professor Reed. 'Generally, they will be started on the cheapest, which might not be the right drug for them.'

Andress was so alarmed by the dangers that she was speaking about her condition as part of The Timeless Women campaign. The aim was to challenge the assumption that osteoporosis was a disease suffered by old ladies, encouraging women of all ages to consider their bone health before it was too late.

'The problem is that there's a lack of awareness among some GPs and members of the public about osteoporosis. They don't think about the health of the bones until a fracture has occurred,' said Professor Reed. The World Health Organisation had introduced a questionnaire called the Frax system, which GPs could use to assess the risk of fracturing a bone due to osteoporosis but it wasn't mandatory. It had been estimated that without changes to the diagnostic system, the number of fractures caused by osteoporosis would double over the following 50 years.

Ursula said, 'I think it's strange that women get told to have a mammogram regularly to check their breasts for cancer, but aren't urged to get their bones checked for osteoporosis. Tragically, many people break bones and are then bed-ridden for a long time, because they didn't know they had the disease. I refuse to become a prisoner of my condition and I urge other women to do the same. Getting older brings lot of strange surprises. It affects your body in ways you don't expect. I have a dog who is getting old and he's losing his hearing, his sight and his capacity for thinking straight. I think this will be me, too, one day, but at least I hope my bones will be OK.'

In 1962 Ursula Andress was one of the most photographed women in the world, following the success of her role as Honey Ryder in the first James Bond film, Dr No. Her opening scene, where she waded out of the Caribbean Sea in a bikini, carrying two large shells, while singing a calypso, had become iconic, having been polled as one of the top 2 'sexiest movie moments' in both the UK and Australia.

At 72 years old she hadn’t lost that film-star aura or her signature eye liner, looking stylish and slightly risqué in a black trouser suit and white ruffled shirt, unbuttoned far enough down to reveal a black bustier. As she looked at her photograph from Dr No, she laughed before saying with her distinctive Swiss accent; "45 years ago looking like that was easy, now it's hard.

These days I prefer a little more darkness, and to keep the old photos going."

An avid collector of art, she said she would only do a film if it was in the name of art, having collaborated with contemporary American artist Matthew Barney, in his film series The Cremaster Cycle: "It has to be art or else I am not interested. There's no shortage of good actors but there's a shortage of good films, because they're very costly, but I did my work, and now I only do things for art."

Ursula divided her time between family in Switzerland and her properties in Rome and the US, joking: "I'm a gypsy, I've always been a gypsy, dreaming about curiosity and dreaming about travelling. The world has become so small today. It's so sad that everything is becoming the same, and different traditions and cultures are all disappearing.

I want to see different cultures, and different traditions, and my favourite places are villages which don't have high-rise houses or cement-block flats, but villages that are confined in a wall with their traditions intact. I did enjoy London in the '60s. Everything was fun, it was a happy town, an English town, but now there are no English there!"

Ten years earlier she'd been diagnosed with osteoporosis, having recently become an ambassador for the prevention of the disease. Andress said that when she was diagnosed, she, like many women, didn't understand the severity of the implications: "It wasn't a shock when I found out, because I didn't know enough about osteoporosis. I was ignorant about the disease. I thought that with calcium tablets and exercise, the bones would get healthier by themselves. I brought a suitcase full of calcium tablets back from America to my home in Rome, because they were cheaper there than in Europe. When my doctor saw them he said Ursula, this alone will not work, so they are now hidden in the cellar of the chateaux."

Even though she knew she had low bone density in her hip, initially, she took her medication lightly: "I'm the worst pill taker in the world; days would go by without me taking the medicine. Now I have a yearly medication and that is much easier for me." The problem, she said, was that it was easy to carry on and feel healthy with osteoporosis.

"Women don't take it seriously enough, because life goes on with osteoporosis very well. There is no pain, you don't feel like you have a disease or sickness, so you do everything – until something cracks. I want to be healthy because I'm very active; I would be miserable staying in bed. I would also be embarrassed and uneasy if someone else had to take care of me. If I can't be active, I want to go."

Andress said that getting older was something nobody could prepare you for: "Age brings you very strange surprises. You know, everybody tells you when you're pregnant, to expect this and to expect that, and it is such a surprise when you discover it for yourself, because it's completely different. It's the same with getting older; aging is a very difficult problem. I have experience, I have knowledge, I have the past - but health can be so problematic."

Ursula had her only child, a son, at the age of 43. "Now there are a lot of mothers who have children at that age, but then it was a scandal. It was a surprise when I found out I was pregnant, because I never thought it was going to happen, but it did, I went with it, and now my son is 28-years-old; it goes so quickly. The only thing that matters when you have children is that of your children's future, but what kind of a world are we leaving the children?"

She said she was fearful of the future and the world we've created, and when asked if she'd ever considered taking up journalism, she replied emphatically in the negative: "No! The injustices of the world are too hard to take in. I'm not very confident at all about the present and future. We've done so many harmful things to nature with pesticides, and 50% of bees have already disappeared." When asked about her personal philosophy, she said; "Maybe you should talk to my son; he majored in philosophy and is a very deep thinker, but my philosophy is to be honest, happy and live life."

spartacuswallpaper.com

Metro Goldwyn Mayer
TRADE
MARK

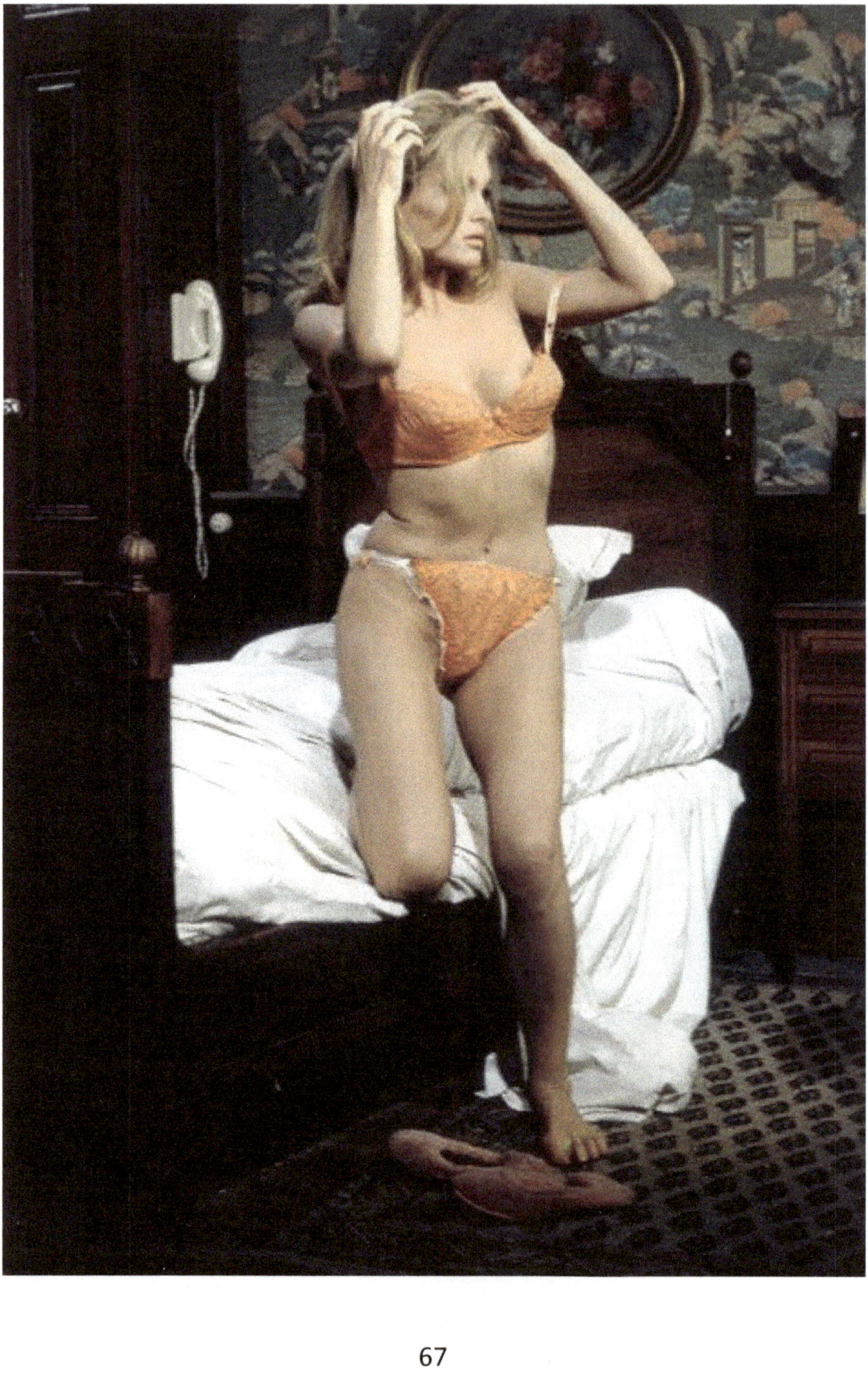

Lightning Source UK Ltd.
Milton Keynes UK
UKHW05f0033241018
331060UK00009B/92/P

9 780464 716976